BEST OF JOHN LEGEND

ISBN 978-1-4803-9375-2

7777 W. BLUEMOUND RD. P.O. BOX 13819 MILWAUKEE, WI 53213

In Australia Contact:
Hal Leonard Australia Pty. Ltd.
4 Lentara Court
Cheltenham, Victoria, 3192 Australia
Email: ausadmin@halleonard.com.au

Visit Hal Leonard Online at
www.halleonard.com

ALL OF ME

Words and Music by JOHN STEPHENS
and TOBY GAD

Moderately, with feeling

What would I do with-out your smart
How man-y times do I have to tell

mouth draw-in' me in and you kick-ing me out? ___ You've got my
you, e-ven when you're cry-ing, you're beau-ti-ful too? ___ The world is

head spin-nin', no kid-din'. I can't pin you down. __
beat-ing you down. I'm __ a-round through ev-er-y mood. __

EVERYBODY KNOWS

Words and Music by JOHN STEPHENS,
TERRENCE SMITH, JAMES HO
and KWAN PRATHER

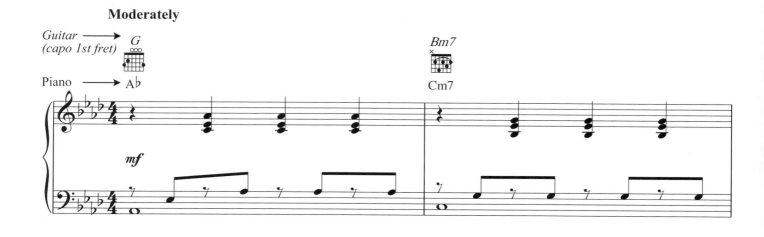

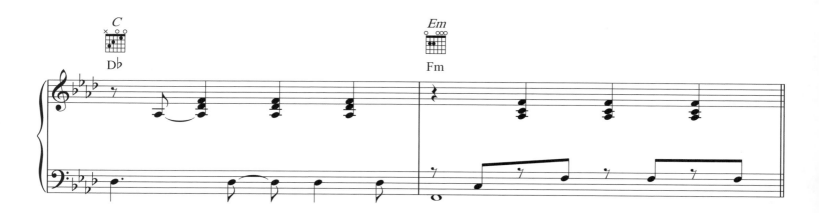

It gets hard- er ev- 'ry day, ___ but I can't seem to shake __ the pain. __
I don't care what the peo- ple say; ___ they're prob-'ly lone- ly an - y - way. __

To Coda

GREEN LIGHT

Words and Music by JOHN STEPHENS,
ANDRE BENJAMIN, JAMES RYAN HO,
RICK NOWELS and FIN GREENALL

MADE TO LOVE

Words and Music by JOHN STEPHENS,
MARSHALL JEFFERSON, KANYE WEST, DAVE TOZER,
MARCOS PALACIOS, ERNEST CLARK, MARVIN BURNS,
KIMBRA JOHNSON, NANA TUFFOUR, JUSTIN BARON
and ANDREW HOROWITZ

*Recorded a half step higher.

made to love. _ (Vocal ad lib.)

ORDINARY PEOPLE

Words and Music by JOHN STEPHENS
and WILL ADAMS

This time we'll take __ it slow. __ Take it __ Take it

slow, _____ slow. _____ This time we'll take __ it

slow. Take it slow, oh, __ oh. _____

This time we'll take __ it slow. _____

rit.   *a tempo*   *dim. e rit.*   *p*

Ped.

SAVE ROOM

Words and Music by JOHN STEPHENS,
WILL ADAMS, JESSICA WILSON,
BUDDY BUIE and JAMES COBB JR.

SLOW DANCE

Words and Music by JOHN STEPHENS,
WILL ADAMS, ESTELLE SWARAY,
LA CHARLES HARPER, RICHARD POINDEXTER
and ROBERT POINDEXTER

(Da, da da, ____ da. ____

Na, na na, ____ na, ____ hoo.) ____

Can we wait just a min-ute, slow it down for a min-ute, now, ba-by? You're
Can we wait just a min-ute, turn that T - V off for a min-ute? That

SO HIGH

Words and Music by JOHN STEPHENS,
DeVON HARRIS, PAUL CHO,
LEON WARE and PAMELA SAWYER

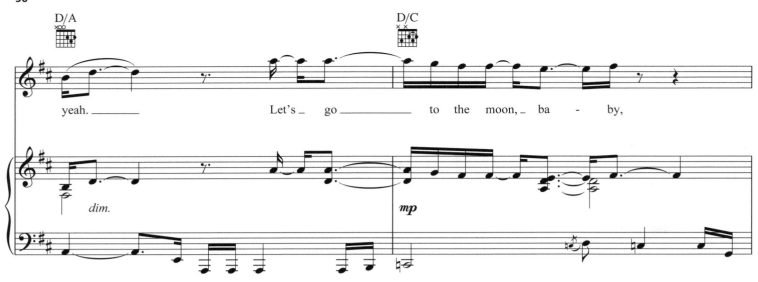

yeah. _____ Let's _ go _____ to the moon,_ ba - by,

dim.   *mp*

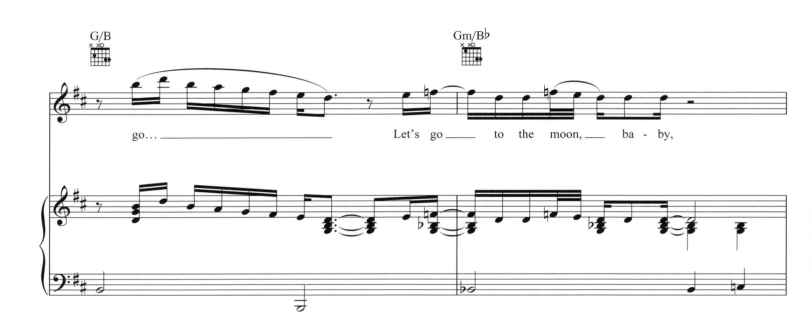

go… _____ Let's go _____ to the moon,_ ba - by,

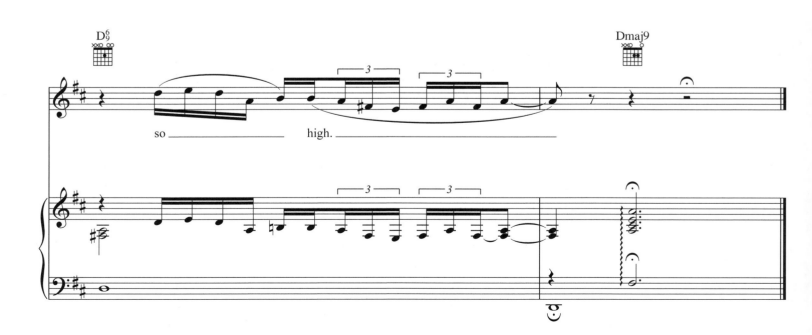

so _____ high. _____

STAY WITH YOU

Words and Music by JOHN STEPHENS
and DAVE TOZER

THIS TIME

Words and Music by JOHN STEPHENS,
KWAN PRATHER and DAVE TOZER

Ran — in-to you yes-ter-day; —
I — hit the bar ev-'ry night —

mem-o-ries rushed — through my —
look-ing to score — a good —

— brain. It's start-ing to hit ____ me, now you're not with __ me. I real-ize I made _ a mis-take.
— time. It's not like I planned _ it. I'm left emp-ty-hand-ed 'cause I'm still a-lone _ in my mind. _

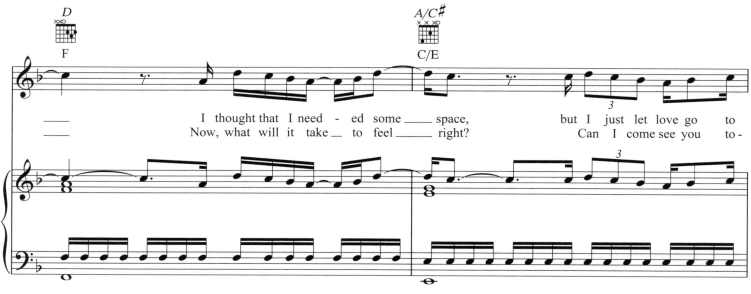

__ I thought that I need - ed some ____ space, but I just let love go to
__ Now, what will it take _ to feel ____ right? Can I come see you to-

waste. It's so cry-stal clear _ now that I need you here _ now. I've got-ta get you back tonight? Is there some-one new _ now? What can I do _ now, 'cause I need you back by my

TONIGHT
(Best You Ever Had)

Words and Music by JOHN STEPHENS,
ALLEN ARTHUR, CLAYTON REILLY,
KEITH JUSTICE, MIGUEL PIMENTAL
and CHRISTOPHER BRIDGES

USED TO LOVE U

Words and Music by JOHN STEPHENS
and KANYE WEST

love __ you.
I ___ don't   love __ you.   Oh, _____ I used __ to   love __ you.

I _____   loved   you. _____   And you gon-na miss me   now, _____
I __ don't   love __ you.)

__ yeah. _____   Ba - by, when I used to   love __ you, ___   there's

WHO DO WE THINK WE ARE

Words and Music by JOHN STEPHENS,
JOSEPH BROUSSARD, CARROL WASHINGTON,
RALPH WILLIAMS, KANYE WEST, MARVIN GAYE,
ED TOWNSEND, DAVE TOZER, ANTHONY KHAN,
GUORDAN BANKS, WILLIAM ROBERTS
and ROOSEVELT HARRELL

Slow R & B groove

We've got a lot of nerve, girl, we walk a-round here like we own this place. See my jewels drip-ping on my Tim-ber-lands, step-ping like a crim-i-nal, suc-cess is so im-mi-nent.

(Spoken:) I don't know about y'all, but I feel good tonight. There's something in the air tonight.

You know, everybody needs someone to look up to. Why shouldn't it be us?

Hey! Who do we think we are? ____

YOU AND I
(Nobody In The World)

Words and Music by JOHN STEPHENS,
DANIEL DODD WILSON, JAMES RYAN HO
and DAVE TOZER

Moderate Ballad

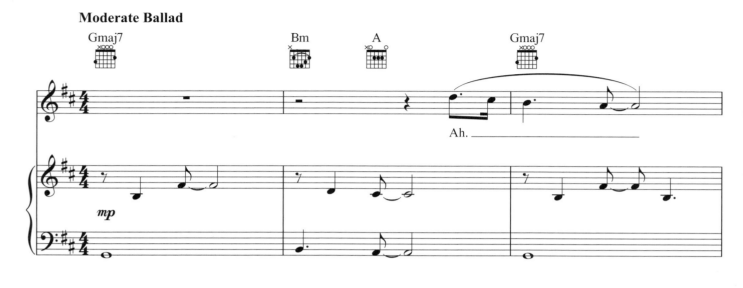